To

_____

From

_____

Date

_____

Get the *Becoming Anchored Companion Journal*

As you go through the Becoming Anchored Devotional, I've designed the Becoming Anchored Companion Journal as a guided resource with prompts for you to dive deeper in your spiritual and personal growth.

The Companion Journal is perfect for those who love to journal additional thoughts or have guidance through study.

Get yours at:
thomasbrattonauthor.com/becoming-anchored-gift

Becoming Anchored

52 Devotionals of Hope for Strengthening Your Faith and Trust in God

Thomas Bratton

Butterfly Books Publishing

Becoming Anchored Devotional
Copyright © Thomas Bratton 2022

Published by Butterfly Books Publishing. Butterfly Books Publishing is an independent publisher.

Cover Design by C5 Designs
Interior Design by Butterfly Books Publishing
Edited and proofread by Jake Waller

Printed in the United States of America

ISBN-13 (e-book): 979-8-9859165-3-9
ISBN-13 (paperback): 979-8-9859165-4-6
ISBN-13 (hardcover): 979-8-9859165-6-0

Contents

What readers have to say:

5 out of 5 stars

"From someone struggling to follow faith consistently, this has opened my eyes again. I'm thankful to have come across his writing at this time in my life. Thank you. I hope this book touches others." – Amazon Reviewer

5 out of 5 stars

"I love that it is a weekly devotional. The content is well laid out. I also love the scripture first, the relatable commentary, the thought-provoking questions, and the extra lined journal page. Very well done!" – Amazon Reviewer

5.0 out of 5 stars

"I am enjoying this so much. Tom is a gifted writer, he has poured his life into *Becoming Anchored*. Practical Bible-based messages that make you think and try to live the life our God intended. Looking forward to giving this as a Christmas present to many this year." – Amazon Reviewer.

BECOMING ANCHORED

"**M**y thoughts are higher than your thoughts sayeth the Lord."

I pray as you meditate on this weekly journey, that your cup overflows with the gift of the Holy Spirit in you. May you be led by hope, steadfast faith in the Lord through honoring Him through others in your daily walk. I hope others see God through you and you would be led to a greater, more fulfilling life of hope, joy, and peace that is greater than anything you have ever experienced before. Let the Holy Spirit be your guide, and the love of Christ be in your hearts forever, in Jesus' name, amen...

HOPE: Hope Opportunity Purpose Encourage

Each weekly devotional is meant to be of hope for yourself and others with opportunities to encourage everyone you encounter by allowing the fruit of the Spirit to become your purpose.

Please use the space after each day to write your thoughts on how the devotional may reflect upon your own life. Write a prayer for you or someone you care about to live life with hope and experience peace which transcends beyond our understanding when we apply God's truths to our lives!

Thomas Bratton

WEEK 1

Whatever are your goals for this week? This month? This year?

How is it going so far with setting goals that align with your values?

Do you allow time for what matters most to you?

What is it you would like to achieve?

Does your faith walk on water?

We hope for the best to come to fruition best through seeking God and His will for us.

Set aside some time to reflect and discover the desires you long for. Ask, "God, are my plans in align with yours?"

In your *Becoming Anchored Companion Journal*, use the prompts and space for your reflections.

Thoughts:

_____

_____

_____

_____

_____

_____

_____

_____

_____

_____

Prayer:

_____

_____

_____

_____

_____

_____

_____

_____

_____

WEEK 2

Don't copy the customs and behaviors of this world, but let God transform you into a new person by changing the way you think. Then you will learn to know God's will for you, which is good and pleasing and perfect.
Romans 12:2 (NLT)

The New Year is a time for new beginnings, resolutions, goals, and change. We all want change, but don't want to take the time, nor make the sacrifices to achieve our desires. Mostly because of fear. Fear of the unknown, fear of change, fear of failure, fear of what others may think, fear of: "Am I doing the right thing?"

Change takes time. Most people don't have goals and only wish their circumstances would change. However, they don't want to change themselves. The first thing to change is how we think. Ask God for His divine will to be done by changing the way you think!

Heavenly Father, I really would love to become a better person, to achieve the desires I have in my heart, which I believe you placed there. Help me to discern what is truly important in my life now, in Jesus' name, Amen.

In your *Becoming Anchored Companion Journal,* use the prompts and space for your reflections.

Thoughts:

_____

_____

_____

_____

_____

_____

_____

_____

_____

_____

Prayer:

_____

_____

_____

_____

_____

_____

_____

_____

_____

WEEK 3

For we are God's masterpiece. He has created us anew in Christ Jesus, so we can do the good things He planned for us a long time ago.
Ephesians 2:10 (NLT)

God is rich in mercy. We know by our own mistakes, yet He is there to help us through our struggles. He examines our hearts and knows our motives.

Have you helped someone in need or done a good deed while hoping for the favor to be returned? Does this sound familiar or are your motives pure? We're not saved because of our good works. But faith is dead without good works. James 2:26

If a woman sees another woman frantic, upsetting as it may be, the best thing she can do is to pray. If God wants you to be of service He will give you the strength and the fortitude to do more in any circumstance.

Faith is what we hope for and hope to be true. It is not self-seeking.

What motives do your intentions reveal?
The world's or God's?

In your *Becoming Anchored Companion Journal,* use the prompts and space for your reflections.

Thoughts:

_____

_____

_____

_____

_____

_____

_____

_____

_____

_____

Prayer:

_____

_____

_____

_____

_____

_____

_____

_____

_____

WEEK 4

But those who hope in the Lord will renew their strength. They will soar on wings like eagles; they will run and not grow weary; they will walk and not be faint.
Isaiah 40:31. (NIV)

God, creator of all things and people, who gives us strength, the beginning of a new day, like the rosy hues of a morning sun rising over the horizon. The glare of the sun on the water and the warmth we feel on our face. His hope is for you to pursue your dreams even when life's circumstances have become overwhelming.

Maybe it's an old dream of yours that hasn't ever seemed to be the right time. A man works his whole life to support his family to avoid the risks of pursuing his dreams. Later in life he may regret he didn't follow those dreams, due to feeling as though he did not have enough time or energy. Whatever the reason may be, today is a new day! You can begin again and pursue those dreams.

Have you any dreams that have not come to pass? Do not be dismayed. **Give them to the Lord and He will give you strength and the will to pursue all things in His name.**

In your *Becoming Anchored Companion Journal*, use the prompts and space for your reflections.

Thoughts:

_____

_____

_____

_____

_____

_____

_____

_____

_____

_____

_____

Prayer:

_____

_____

_____

_____

_____

_____

_____

_____

_____

_____

WEEK 5

See, I will do a new thing. It will begin happening now. Will you not know about it? I will even make a road in the wilderness, and rivers in the desert.
Isaiah 43:19 (NLV)

I saiah writes in chapter 43 v.18 to forget the former things. Do not dwell on them. Good or bad. I have focused on the thought, *'If I would have done this a different way, maybe things would be better.'* Well, it's a little late to change the past. God doesn't want us to hash over the past, feel shameful or feel regrets.

Therefore, Isaiah goes on to talk about what God is doing now. And if we miss it because we're still in the past, then what would our future be like? More importantly, what about today?

Focus on today, for today is the "day the Lord hath made."

Lord, help me to keep my eyes and thoughts focused on today, where I can seek you and your kingdom, Amen.

What do you need to let go of from the past which keeps you from today?

In your *Becoming Anchored Companion Journal,* use the prompts and space for your reflections.

Thoughts:

_____

_____

_____

_____

_____

_____

_____

_____

_____

_____

Prayer:

_____

_____

_____

_____

_____

_____

_____

_____

_____

WEEK 6

*If I gave everything I have to the poor and even sacrificed my body, I could boast
about it; but if I didn't love others, I would have gained nothing.*
1 Corinthians 13:3 (NLT)

We should love one another. 1 John 3:11 (NLT)

Thank the Lord for all He has done for you. Giving comes from
a loving heart. Not just to your family and friends, but to
everyone, even people who have done wrong by you!

That my friend is unconditional love.

My hope is that through the coming weeks you'll love others as
you love yourself. A thought may be to give some of your time or
other resources and to extend your love to one of God's children.
Donate to your Church. Volunteer to a cause you believe in. Help a
neighbor.

Heavenly Father, thank you for your unconditional love that
inspires me to love. Help me to love others as you see them, and not
think of myself as better than they are. In Jesus' name, Amen.

God loves you unconditionally.
Do you give unconditionally?

In your *Becoming Anchored Companion Journal,* use the prompts and
space for your reflections.

Thoughts:

_____

_____

_____

_____

_____

_____

_____

_____

_____

_____

Prayer:

_____

_____

_____

_____

_____

_____

_____

_____

_____

WEEK 7

Let's not merely say that we love each other; let us show the truth by our actions.
1 John 3:18 (NLT)

Don't leave it up to someone else to help somebody in need. Jesus said, "The poor will always be among you."

If you have money, share it with someone who is struggling. Don't expect them to pay you back interest but hope they too will pay it forward by sharing their gifts. Everyone has something they can share: a meal with someone who is hungry, a kind word an affirmation to someone who is lonely or depressed.

The importance of giving is your love and your time! Not just money.

If you're not sure where to start, Pray, ask friends and families for ideas, and your Church family. Ask, seek, and knock!

What do you have to share today?

In your *Becoming Anchored Companion Journal,* use the prompts and space for your reflections.

Thoughts:

_____

_____

_____

_____

_____

_____

_____

_____

_____

_____

Prayer:

_____

_____

_____

_____

_____

_____

_____

_____

_____

_____

WEEK 8

For God loved the world so much that he gave his one and only Son, so that everyone who believes in him will not perish but have eternal life.
John 3:16 (NLT)

Love is patient and kind. Love is not jealous or boastful or proud or rude. It does not demand its own way. It is not irritable, and it keeps no record of being wronged.
1 Corinthians 13:4-5 (NLT)

G od's gift to us is His love. Not to judge or condemn us! All things come from Him who lives in us for His great love for you and me.

Be kind to one another, do not judge, pray for others! Always remember to share God's love for you with someone else. Offer to pray with someone. Giving hope is one of the kindest things you can offer. Pray to help everyone, even people who are on a different path than yourself. Be kind and compassionate to everyone.

Plant those seeds of prayer and see what God does next.

How does your love reveal Godly love in your daily journey?

In your *Becoming Anchored Companion Journal,* use the prompts and space for your reflections.

Thoughts:

_____

_____

_____

_____

_____

_____

_____

_____

_____

_____

Prayer:

_____

_____

_____

_____

_____

_____

_____

_____

WEEK 9

*For God saved us and called us to live a **Holy** life. He did this, not because we deserved it, but because that was his plan from the beginning of time—to show us his grace through Christ Jesus.*
2 Timothy 1:9 (NLT)

God's plan for us is to live a Holy life, which may include sacrifices. For example, a guest staying with you in your home. Do you want them to feel at home or do you just say that and feel a different way? Whatever the situation might be, let it be in God's Honor by honoring your guests with grace, dignity, and respect.

My wife and I stay in bed and breakfast inns often. It's difficult to feel comfortable in someone else's home at times. I am always hopeful to feel comfortable wherever I may be away from home and am grateful for the hosts grace for sharing their home.

Have you opened your home "heart" to someone in love?

What sacrifices might you make this week?

Do you begrudge any hostilities that keep you from showing grace?

In your *Becoming Anchored Companion Journal,* use the prompts and space for your reflections.

Thoughts:

_____

_____

_____

_____

_____

_____

_____

_____

_____

_____

_____

Prayer:

_____

_____

_____

_____

_____

_____

_____

_____

_____

_____

WEEK 10

But his wife said, "If the LORD were going to kill us, he wouldn't have accepted our burnt offering and grain offering. He wouldn't have appeared to us and told us this wonderful thing and done these miracles."
Judges 13:23 (NLT)

Born to Manoah and his wife, a son, Samson, went on to become one of the strongest men in history, conquering hundreds of men in his destruction. Samson's sexual desires had often rendered him weak and eventually led to death.

Like Samson, many of us have addictive behaviors, alcohol, drugs, food disorders, and the list goes on. We can overcome our addictions when we have surrendered to the will of God. For it is the hope each of us becomes a better person. These may be opportunities to help others who have suffered similar addictive behaviors.

What behaviors do you need to surrender?

In your *Becoming Anchored Companion Journal*, use the prompts and space for your reflections.

Thoughts:

_____

_____

_____

_____

_____

_____

_____

_____

_____

_____

Prayer:

_____

_____

_____

_____

_____

_____

_____

_____

_____

WEEK 11

He renews my strength. He guides me along right paths, bringing honor to his name.
Psalms 23:3 (NLT)

There are times that we may follow a different path than what God has planned for us. For God has given us free will. He will always be near if you seek Him.

The lake waters are roughest blowing in the direction of the shore. At any time, He can direct the winds in a different direction, bringing calmness to the seas. He parted the red sea for the Israelites during their escape from slavery. He will do the same for you too. Being obedient to God is the path of least resistance.

Let go and let God direct your paths and make them straight. Obedience prepares us for servanthood, for God blesses those that obey Him as He invites you to share your blessings with others.

Which path have you chosen to follow?
How has God renewed your strength?

In your *Becoming Anchored Companion Journal*, use the prompts and space for your reflections.

Thoughts:

_____

_____

_____

_____

_____

_____

_____

_____

_____

_____

_____

Prayer:

_____

_____

_____

_____

_____

_____

_____

_____

_____

WEEK 12

And I know it is important to love him with all my heart and all my understanding and all my strength, and to love my neighbor as myself. This is more important than to offer all of the burnt offerings and sacrifices required in the law.
Mark 12:33 (NIV)

Today, God wants people to make sacrifices, but the sacrifice He wants us to make is out of love. To love God and to love His people. Always find the good in others. Get to know others; listen to their stories. There is no better way to get to know someone than by simply listening. Being there is brings hope, listening helps others feel valued and that they matter. How do you feel when someone listens to you?

Does expressing that kind of tender-hearted love really involve a sacrifice?

How will you manifest love this week?

In your *Becoming Anchored Companion Journal,* use the prompts and space for your reflections.

Thoughts:

_____

_____

_____

_____

_____

_____

_____

_____

_____

_____

Prayer:

_____

_____

_____

_____

_____

_____

_____

_____

WEEK 13

I am the good shepherd. The good shepherd sacrifices his life for the sheep.
John 10:11 (NLT)

J esus endured the ultimate sacrifice so we may live, freeing us from the penalties of sins so we may be saved.

Parents often protect their children from harm and endure the consequences themselves. Sometimes those sacrifices are to protect them and then there are times we make sacrifices that provide opportunities for them. Some parents make financial sacrifices to send their children to college, furthering their education.

Maybe a family member is having a difficult time and you invite them to stay in your home. Or maybe a friend is struggling, and you offer to help them with their situation.

We're not trying to enable anyone, and yet we all go through challenging times, it may be inconvenient, we may feel unable to help. Showing our love for them may require some sacrifices. While giving them hope and feeling adequate, loved, and respected.

What sacrifices have you made for your family? How did it feel? Has anyone made such sacrifices for you out of love?

In your *Becoming Anchored Companion Journal,* use the prompts and space for your reflections.

Thoughts:

_____

_____

_____

_____

_____

_____

_____

_____

_____

_____

Prayer:

_____

_____

_____

_____

_____

_____

_____

_____

WEEK 14

Don't worry about anything; instead, pray about everything. Tell God what you need and thank him for all he has done. Then you will experience God's peace, which exceeds anything we can understand. His peace will guard your hearts and minds as you live in Christ Jesus.
Philippians 4:6-7 (NLT)

W hen you wake in the morning it may be easy to succumb to your daily routine. This may happen day after day, week after week, until you come to the realization that nothing changes if nothing changes. This transformation will only come from your willingness to surrender to change. Don't give in; instead, submit your schedule, your life to God. And thank Him for leading you along the path that He has destined for you to follow. When you get into harmony with God, you will soon experience true tranquility and peacefulness beyond all human understating.

Have you made your requests known to God and thanked Him for all He has done?

In your *Becoming Anchored Companion Journal,* use the prompts and space for your reflections.

Thoughts:

_____

_____

_____

_____

_____

_____

_____

_____

_____

_____

Prayer:

_____

_____

_____

_____

_____

_____

_____

_____

_____

_____

WEEK 15

Neither our fears for today nor our worries about tomorrow—not even the powers of hell can separate us from God's love.
Romans 8:38 (NLT)

Why do our fears expel worry about things we cannot control? We know that God is in control and has the power to work everything accordingly to those who surrender to and love Him. Hoping for an outcome, for tomorrow to improve, or for the sun to shine so the family may enjoy the day at the beach is all fine, but when you become obsessed with tomorrow, it's time to let go of those worries and remember; Do not worry about tomorrow, for tomorrow will be here soon enough, today has its own troubles. Matthew 6:34

We all have plans for tomorrow, or some other time in the future, but we get there one day at a time!

Have you committed yourself to God completely? Do you trust Him?

Focus upon this day and let God worry about tomorrow.

In your *Becoming Anchored Companion Journal,* use the prompts and space for your reflections.

Thoughts:

_____

_____

_____

_____

_____

_____

_____

_____

_____

_____

_____

Prayer:

_____

_____

_____

_____

_____

_____

_____

_____

_____

WEEK 16

Be still and know that I am God.
Psalms 46:10 (NIV)

Taking time for self-care is so important. To our heart, our mind, and our soul. I often go for walks, sometimes along the water's edge, yet sometimes in the woods following the path before me. I think to myself, *'I chose to stay on this path. Why is it so difficult to follow the path God has chosen for me?'* Soon I come to the end of my walk and feel relaxed, rejuvenated, and ready to continue on with the day ahead.

Later I may ask myself, *'What happened back there? Did I miss something? Maybe there was a message, but I don't remember what it was.'* Then I reflect upon the day and soon realize this is the day the Lord hath made, I shall rejoice and be glad in it. I feel at peace with myself and my surroundings and soon have determined the message. 'Be still and know that I am God!' All I needed was to reflect upon Him, and know He is in control.

Where is your sanctuary?

In your *Becoming Anchored Companion Journal,* use the prompts and space for your reflections.

Thoughts:

_____

_____

_____

_____

_____

_____

_____

_____

_____

_____

_____

Prayer:

_____

_____

_____

_____

_____

_____

_____

_____

_____

_____

_____

_____

WEEK 17

For by grace, you have been saved through faith, and that not of yourselves; it is the gift of God, not of works, lest anyone should boast.
Ephesians 2:8-9 (NKJV)

Grace is receiving more than we deserve, not by doing good deeds. It is with humility. We are grateful and through our faith, our desire is to shower others with kindness, generosity and out of love. God blesses us in many ways, like restoring a relationship with a friend or sibling, a better job, a promotion. He also gives us our own unique skills and talents so we may use them to serve others. God is pleased when we share our gifts with others. It gives Him great pleasure to bless us with exceptional gifts, and talents.

Thank you, Lord, for all you have done for me and my family, there's no way I can repay you or outgive you, but know this God, I will keep your ways and your commands in my heart with joy in Jesus' name, Amen.

In what manner will you demonstrate grace to someone you know? Or who you don't know?

In your *Becoming Anchored Companion Journal,* use the prompts and space for your reflections.

Thoughts:

_____

_____

_____

_____

_____

_____

_____

_____

_____

_____

_____

Prayer:

_____

_____

_____

_____

_____

_____

_____

_____

_____

_____

WEEK 18

Therefore, as God's chosen people, holy and dearly loved, clothe yourselves with
compassion, kindness, humility, gentleness, and patience.
Colossians 3:12 (NIV)

Distractions are merely stumbling blocks to keep us in alignment with how we respond to the world. It is important to not be so hasty in aligning ourselves with the world as we know it today. These days we've been hit hard. The pandemic and its effect on the world. What's a person to do? Rant and rave or respond as God does with his overflowing grace, mercy, and unconditional love? Maybe we are to learn how to slow down and not think of ourselves with such high regard. Humble yourselves before responding to the co-worker who is constantly needing your help. Help them!

On your way home, you stop at the store and people are unthoughtful, hurried, and rude. Smile and wish them a good day!

Once your home, don't complain. Just breathe and thank God you arrived home safely.

Look for the good in everyone, even when you're in a hurry. Be kind, show mercy to those who may take advantage of you, and be graceful to everyone. That may be God speaking to you; slow down, take the higher road. Those others are on a different path and likely having a difficult time through all this.

How would you like to be regarded? The same holds true for everyone.

In your *Becoming Anchored Companion Journal,* use the prompts and space for your reflections.

Thoughts:

_____

_____

_____

_____

_____

_____

_____

_____

_____

_____

_____

Prayer:

_____

_____

_____

_____

_____

_____

_____

_____

_____

WEEK 19

But because of his great love for us, God, who is rich in mercy, made us alive with Christ even when we were dead in transgressions—it is by grace you have been saved.
Ephesians 2:4-5 (NIV)

There are similarities between mercy and grace, "God's love for us".

Mercy is not getting what we deserve. Grace is receiving more than what we deserve.

While we have all fallen on difficult times, we can all appreciate God's love for us. Have you put yourself in someone's else's shoes? I mean really tried. It's not easy! The adult child who comes home because they lost their job and can no longer make it on their own. Your next-door neighbor is working from home as many of us are these days, and they complain to you about all the noise coming from your home. Many have swallowed their pride during this pandemic and humbled themselves. Maybe you're worried about enabling them, or are you becoming untied? Be kind, be prayerful!

Maybe it's time to start a gratitude list? Then you'll feel those knots go away and show the grace we all hope for during challenging times.

In your *Becoming Anchored Companion Journal,* use the prompts and space for your reflections.

Thoughts:

_____
_____
_____
_____
_____
_____
_____
_____
_____
_____

Prayer:

_____
_____
_____
_____
_____
_____
_____
_____
_____
_____

WEEK 20

As you know, we count as blessed those who have persevered. You have heard of Job's perseverance and have seen what the Lord finally brought about. The Lord is full of compassion and mercy.
James 5:11 (NIV)

The Bible conveys how numerous people have endured difficulties in their lives and were later exalted. There are countless people who have gone through the very same thing you are going through now. Joseph endured loneliness, was sold into slavery, yet he didn't hold any grudges. Paul was a murderer, a criminal at large. Today someone such as Paul would be in prison for life. But through God's mercy and compassion He used Paul to do great things, despite being shipwrecked, imprisoned and more. God will do the same for you too, as He has done for others.

Think about some times you have been extended mercy.
Is there anyone in your life now who deserves the same?
Maybe there's someone at work or at church who could use some compassion right now.

In your *Becoming Anchored Companion Journal,* use the prompts and space for your reflections.

Thoughts:

_____
_____
_____
_____
_____
_____
_____
_____
_____
_____

Prayer:

_____
_____
_____
_____
_____
_____
_____
_____
_____

WEEK 21

So, let's not get tired of doing what is good. At just the right time we will reap a harvest of blessing if we don't give up.
Galatians 6:9. (NLT)

Each day is an opportunity to start again. Or maybe change something! Do not grow weary; for if you persevere, you will reap the rewards you are seeking in due time.

Sometimes we may expect instant gratification as we live in an "I want it and I want it now" world. The best things come to those who are determined and willing to make sacrifices.

Think of a farmer who plants the seeds in the spring and harvests the crop in the fall. What about the expectant mother, for instance, Mary, waiting to give birth to Jesus. A friend of mine had planted hundreds of pine trees a couple decades ago, no more than a few inches tall. Years later, he allowed me to use one for a Christmas tree. There are so many opportunities for you to be of service. Be thankful for those opportunities!

What seeds have you planted?

In your *Becoming Anchored Companion Journal*, use the prompts and space for your reflections.

Thoughts:

_____

_____

_____

_____

_____

_____

_____

_____

_____

_____

_____

Prayer:

_____

_____

_____

_____

_____

_____

_____

_____

_____

_____

WEEK 22

If you remain in me and my words remain in you, you may ask for anything
you want, and it will be granted!
John 15:7. (NLT)

C ountless times we try to do things our own way and allow our pride to decide what is best for us. We make relational decisions, financial decisions, spiritual decisions, and endless other decisions; but have you ever asked the one whom can give you your heart's desire?

And don't just ask Him but thank Him for all He has done and is going to do. He will guide you and move mountains to the end of the earth if what you are asking for is within His purposes.

Do your desires align with God's will for you?

In your *Becoming Anchored Companion Journal*, use the prompts and space for your reflections.

Thoughts:

_____

_____

_____

_____

_____

_____

_____

_____

_____

_____

_____

Prayer:

_____

_____

_____

_____

_____

_____

_____

_____

_____

_____

WEEK 23

"Keep on asking, and you will receive what you ask for. Keep on seeking, and
you will find. Keep on knocking, and the door will be opened to you. For
everyone who asks, receives. Everyone who seeks, finds. And to everyone who
knocks, the door will be opened."
Luke 7: 7-8 (NLT)

The Gospel says to keep on searching. What are you searching for? The Lord will provide for you. He will give you strength and encouragement so you may encourage others. And He will open doors to new and better opportunities that no one can shut. Ask Him for anything in Jesus' name, and watch what God does next!

Heavenly Father, thank you for all you have done, thank you for the opportunities that are before me, and I thank you for all the people you have placed in my life. Please hear what I'm about to say, I know I have free will, that sometimes has worked against me, I pray you would open the right doors for me as I try to overcome the hurdles I have been struggling with for so long, in Jesus' name.

What are you asking and seeking for? Have you knocked on the right doors?

In your *Becoming Anchored Companion Journal,* use the prompts and space for your reflections.

Thoughts:

_____

_____

_____

_____

_____

_____

_____

_____

_____

_____

Prayer:

_____

_____

_____

_____

_____

_____

_____

_____

_____

WEEK 24

For God presented Jesus as the sacrifice for sin. People are made right with God when they believe that Jesus sacrificed his life, shedding his blood. This sacrifice shows that God was being fair when he held back and did not punish those who sinned in times past.
Romans 3:25 (NLT)

A bove all things we hope for is the hope of salvation, through the faith we have from when Jesus lived on earth so that we may be saved. We can enjoy the life He has given to us every day. God wants us to enjoy life and to share the good news with others, bringing joy into their lives. What more could we hope for? God already supplied all our needs.

We have many needs, but let's not confuse them with our wants. Keep hope alive by sharing your blessings with others. The gifts we have are meant to give away. There is no greater joy in life! My hope is for you to share your passions, your joys and what God is doing in your life right now.

Have you shared your joy in the Lord with others? Your hopes? Your aspirations?

In your *Becoming Anchored Companion Journal,* use the prompts and space for your reflections.

Thoughts:

_____

_____

_____

_____

_____

_____

_____

_____

_____

_____

Prayer:

_____

_____

_____

_____

_____

_____

_____

_____

_____

WEEK 25

Without a doubt, we all make mistakes from time to time. How we respond is either a reflection of ourselves or that according to God's image as He perceives us. Conversely, it would be to our advantage to let go of our past mistakes and press forward. God does not hold us back from following our dreams, but reliving the past failures will hold you back from everything God has planned for you.

For me, I keep making some of the same mistakes repeatedly. Like the Israelites on their quest for the promised land. It can be a constant battle. Maybe you can relate to this or know someone who struggles in this area. It is alright to think about the past, but then let it go, it is when we harbor those thoughts that holds us back from everything God has planned for you.

What is keeping you from your dreams?

In your *Becoming Anchored Companion Journal,* use the prompts and space for your reflections.

Thoughts:

_____

_____

_____

_____

_____

_____

_____

_____

_____

_____

_____

Prayer:

_____

_____

_____

_____

_____

_____

_____

_____

_____

WEEK 26

I don't mean to say that I have already achieved these things or that I have already reached perfection. But I press on to possess that perfection for which Christ Jesus first possessed me. No, dear brothers and sisters, I have not achieved it, but I focus on this one thing: Forgetting the past and looking forward to what lies ahead, I press on to reach the end of the race and receive the heavenly prize for which God, through Christ Jesus, is calling us.
Philippians 3:12-14 (NLT)

L ife is a journey, not a destination. Although we may perceive how we would like things to become, first we must let go of the past. Living in the past or the future is not living where Jesus lives. He lives in the present. Only God knows what the future holds.

What do you need to let go of from the past so you can move forward?

Pray for God's divine grace and discernment. Focus upon what He has placed in your heart. Soon you will recognize God's divine plans for you. Those plans may not be as you had once hoped for, but don't be dismayed because they will be better than you would have ever imagined!

In your *Becoming Anchored Companion Journal,* use the prompts and space for your reflections.

Thoughts:

_____

_____

_____

_____

_____

_____

_____

_____

_____

_____

Prayer:

_____

_____

_____

_____

_____

_____

_____

_____

_____

WEEK 27

Worry leads you nowhere. Focus on the Lord; think of what is honorable, just, and right. Positive thinking creates positive results, praying promotes hope, and hope is the foundation of peace that begets joy. The troubles we have in a day are enough for one day. Rejoice in the Lord!

Does your worry keep you from focusing on your dreams? Let them go! Write them down and forget them. Many times, the worries we have are meaningless and you'll soon notice how God works everything for the good!

How has letting go of worry resulted in positivity for everything you have hoped for?

In your *Becoming Anchored Companion Journal,* use the prompts and space for your reflections.

Thoughts:

_____
_____
_____
_____
_____
_____
_____
_____
_____
_____
_____

Prayer:

_____
_____
_____
_____
_____
_____
_____
_____
_____
_____
_____

WEEK 28

Seek the Kingdom of God above all else, and live righteously, and he will give you everything you need.
Matthew 6:33 (NLT)

L et your requests be known to the Lord and earnestly seek His will in all you do! Think of all the times God has come to your rescue, opened doors for you, and given you with strength to carry on when you didn't think you could. Even better, write down all He has done for you. You won't be disappointed! Meditate on this for the next week and listen attentively to what the Lord has to show you.

Do you notice how your desires align with what God has already done for you?

In your *Becoming Anchored Companion Journal*, use the prompts and space for your reflections.

Thoughts:

_____

_____

_____

_____

_____

_____

_____

_____

_____

_____

_____

Prayer:

_____

_____

_____

_____

_____

_____

_____

_____

_____

_____

WEEK 29

Trust in the Lord with all your heart and lean not on your own understanding;
in all ways submit to Him, and He will make your paths straight.
Proverbs 3:5-6 (NIV)

We don't know what today is going to bring. Sometimes circumstances go one way, leaving us to wonder, *'Now what?'* Then again, something wonderful may come along which is totally unexpected yet welcome. Therefore, it may be difficult to place too much hope in ourselves without leaning upon the Lord. We simply cannot think of every scenario. When our hope is the Lord, our faith will carry us through any storm that may come our way.

When the disciples were on their boat, there came along a storm. Water was coming into the boat; they were all frightened; it was dark; "Will the boat sink?" one of them asked. They tried to bail water as fast as they could while Jesus was asleep. Soon Jesus awakened and said, "Ye of little faith," and ordered the winds to subside. He calmed the disciples and their fears.

Have you submitted your fears to the Lord?

How has placing your trust in Jesus made your path possible?

In your *Becoming Anchored Companion Journal,* use the prompts and space for your reflections.

Thoughts:

_____

_____

_____

_____

_____

_____

_____

_____

_____

_____

_____

Prayer:

_____

_____

_____

_____

_____

_____

_____

_____

_____

WEEK 30

Love never gives up, never loses faith, is always hopeful, and endures through
every circumstance.
1 Corinthians 13:7 (NLT)

Jesus is with you in every circumstance; "He will never leave you or forsake you", just call His name. Do you know someone that is struggling? Show them that hope is sustained through faith. Don't be afraid to share how God has led you through adversities. Just as He led the Israelites out of slavery to the promised land, He too will guide you, if you take the first step of faith. Peter got out of the boat to meet Jesus, while he was focused on Jesus, he was doing just fine walking on the water, it was only when Peter took his eyes off Jesus he began to sink. Faith, hope, and love can and will cover a multitude of sins. As it has for many before. God didn't give up on us, He gave us the gift of Jesus, therefore, keep on keeping on.

How is your hope intertwined with faith? And love?

In your *Becoming Anchored Companion Journal*, use the prompts and space for your reflections.

Thoughts:

_____

_____

_____

_____

_____

_____

_____

_____

_____

_____

Prayer:

_____

_____

_____

_____

_____

_____

_____

_____

_____

WEEK 31

And we know that in all things God works for the good of those who love him,
who have been called according to his purpose.
Romans 8:28 (NIV)

You may be going through a difficult time now, feeling overwhelmed and stressed. Our hope is God will bring good out of everything. He allows the adversities to occur so we may bless others with the knowledge and talents we possess. As a result, the sacrifices we make will be a blessing to others, not in anticipation of being rewarded; servanthood is our reward.

Lord I'm so grateful for not giving up on me when I was ready to throw in the towel, but you threw it back and gave me another chance. All I had to do was follow you, in Jesus' name, Amen.

How do the sacrifices you make to help others work for the good of them and yourself?

In your *Becoming Anchored Companion Journal,* use the prompts and space for your reflections.

Thoughts:

_____

_____

_____

_____

_____

_____

_____

_____

_____

_____

Prayer:

_____

_____

_____

_____

_____

_____

_____

_____

_____

WEEK 32

Fix your thoughts on what is true, and honorable, and right, and pure, and lovely, and admirable. Think about things that are excellent and worthy of praise.
Philippians 4:8 9 (NLT)

E very day there is a multitude of distractions that may cause us to feel anxious, fearful, and leave us feeling a sense of hopelessness when our attention is focused on what is wrong. And many times, we imagine things are worse than they are.

Sit quietly and count your blessings. This may take some time, but if you persist, the Lord will meet you there. Keep a positive outlook with an attitude of gratitude. You too will experience a peace that is beyond understanding. Anytime you feel stuck with negative reflections, reach out in prayer with thankfulness.

What are you grateful for?

The more you focus on your blessings, the easier it is to let go of the distractions clouding your mind.

In your *Becoming Anchored Companion Journal,* use the prompts and space for your reflections.

Thoughts:

_____

_____

_____

_____

_____

_____

_____

_____

_____

_____

_____

Prayer:

_____

_____

_____

_____

_____

_____

_____

_____

_____

WEEK 33

With man this is impossible, but with God all things are possible.
Matthew 19:26 (NIV)

While we still try to solve our own problems; God can turn our problems into blessings. Simply by asking for discernment, opportunities will arise; you will be in the right place at the right time. Don't allow your hopes to be a selfless act of your own desires. Live in accordance with God's will and He will give you the true desires of your heart.

I've learned through the years, the more I play it safe, the longer it takes for my dreams to come to fruition. Sometimes because of fear, other times from not making the necessary sacrifices to the next plateau. Don't let this be you! Make the time. Take the risk. God is waiting for you there.

Are your goals in alignment with God's divine purpose for you?

In your *Becoming Anchored Companion Journal,* use the prompts and space for your reflections.

Thoughts:

_____

_____

_____

_____

_____

_____

_____

_____

_____

_____

_____

Prayer:

_____

_____

_____

_____

_____

_____

_____

_____

_____

_____

_____

WEEK 34

This is the Day that the Lord has made. Let us be full of joy and be glad in it.
Psalms 118:24 (NLV)

The Lord says today is the day. Not tomorrow or the day after, or maybe sometime next week. This is where you will find God in the present. So why be anxious for tomorrow? Let go of your worries and enjoy today.

Maybe you have heard in recovery, "One day at a time"? Recovering alcoholics don't think about if they might pick up a drink this weekend. No, they simply stay in the moment. After all, this is all we have; tomorrow is not promised. We can find hope today and be glad in it.

If all you can do is all you can do today, then what more is there to do: worry, or take notice of how glorious today is.

Therefore, if we hope for things to come in the future, then we must be present today!

Where is your hope?

What are you joyful for today?

In your *Becoming Anchored Companion Journal,* use the prompts and space for your reflections.

Thoughts:

_____

_____

_____

_____

_____

_____

_____

_____

_____

_____

Prayer:

_____

_____

_____

_____

_____

_____

_____

_____

_____

_____

WEEK 35

"Come to me, all of you who are weary and carry heavy burdens, and I will give you rest."
Matthew 11:28 (NIV)

We become weighed down by our transgressions, finding it difficult to find hope. How much better would you feel knowing God can turn your problems into blessings? He has promised to give you hope when you seek Him with all your heart, and in doing so you will be at peace knowing you don't carry those burdens alone. Always going from one difficulty to another can be daunting. Do you need a time out from life's difficulties? The circumstances we often worry about are not as bad as worrying about them.

Almighty Father, I am so glad to have you by my side. You said you would never leave me, that you have good plans for me, and you would work everything out for the good. Please, Father, help me through this difficult time, if it must be, then, please give me the strength and fortitude to get through this, in Jesus' name, Amen.

What burdens are you carrying?

In your *Becoming Anchored Companion Journal,* use the prompts and space for your reflections.

Thoughts:

_____

_____

_____

_____

_____

_____

_____

_____

_____

_____

_____

Prayer:

_____

_____

_____

_____

_____

_____

_____

_____

WEEK 36

We have been beaten, been put in prison, faced angry mobs, worked to exhaustion, endured sleepless nights, and gone without food.
2 Corinthians 6:5 (NLT)

C onsider the acronym HALT: "hungry, angry, lonely, and tired". Helplessness is when the evil one is prowling around to make his presence known. Fight back like the Apostle Paul; imprisoned during much of his ministry, shipwrecked, and yet he fought the good fight. He pressed on and did not look back. Many times, God will use the challenges we endure to bless us, or He may be using us to be a blessing to someone else. So, remember to HALT the next time you are hungry, angry, lonely, or tired; and seek God first, and all things shall be added unto you. Hope never ends, never gives in!

When have you needed to use the acronym HALT in your life?

In your *Becoming Anchored Companion Journal*, use the prompts and space for your reflections.

Thoughts:

_____

_____

_____

_____

_____

_____

_____

_____

_____

_____

_____

Prayer:

_____

_____

_____

_____

_____

_____

_____

_____

_____

_____

WEEK 37

Jesus went to the grave with a sad heart. The grave was a hole on the side of a hill. A stone covered the door. "Roll the stone aside," Jesus told them.
John 11:38-39 (NLV)

The story of the death of Lazarus teaches us to be steadfast in our faith. His mercy never ends, so why shall we worry, be angry and frustrated, or give up? Hope is the expectation for things that are not yet seen, and the faith we have when we believe. Trust in the Lord and do not lean on your own understanding. If you are angry, remember the acronym HALT, and let Jesus roll the stone aside to free you from your anguish.

Keep your thoughts focused on Jesus. Peter walked on water when he kept his eyes focused upon Jesus.

What can you ask Jesus to roll away in your life right now?

In your *Becoming Anchored Companion Journal,* use the prompts and space for your reflections.

Thoughts:

_____

_____

_____

_____

_____

_____

_____

_____

_____

_____

Prayer:

_____

_____

_____

_____

_____

_____

_____

_____

_____

WEEK 38

Be strong and courageous. Do not be afraid; do not be discouraged, for the LORD your God will be with you wherever you go.
Joshua 1:9 (NLT)

When frustrated, angry, and tired, we often become consumed with anxiety and feel threatened. Acknowledge your weakness and say, "Jesus help me." Let go of your will and ask the Lord for His will to be done, that your actions and words would be pleasing to Him. Ask for a favorable outcome to the circumstances which are troubling you so they will not be overwhelming. God is the source of all strength, hope, and love.

Have you read how Joshua brought the Israelites into the promised land?

How will you be more courageous like Joshua?

In your *Becoming Anchored Companion Journal,* use the prompts and space for your reflections.

Thoughts:

_____

_____

_____

_____

_____

_____

_____

_____

_____

_____

Prayer:

_____

_____

_____

_____

_____

_____

_____

_____

_____

WEEK 39

Shouldn't you have mercy on your fellow servant, just as I had mercy on you?
That's what my heavenly Father will do to you if you refuse to forgive your
brothers and sisters from your heart.
Matthew 18:33,35 (NIV)

There is an old saying: "What goes around comes around." When we have lessons to learn, this statement is like déjà vu. Do you recall a time when you were not particularly kind and later similar events occurred that ignited your memory as you were shown no mercy, love, or forgiveness?

Treat others as you would like to be treated. Three things will last forever: faith, hope, and love, and love is the greatest of all these.

Lord, help me to forgive others as you have forgiven me. Let me see them through your eyes and bless them as you have blessed me, in Jesus' name, Amen.

Do you treat others as you want to be treated? Why or why not?

In your *Becoming Anchored Companion Journal,* use the prompts and space for your reflections.

Thoughts:

_____

_____

_____

_____

_____

_____

_____

_____

_____

_____

_____

Prayer:

_____

_____

_____

_____

_____

_____

_____

_____

_____

_____

WEEK 40

When troubles come your way, consider it an opportunity for great joy.
James 1:2 (NIV)

L ife's journey can be difficult during times of adversity. Consider it an opportunity which may test your faith. God did not intend us to live in fear. Therefore, be bold and courageous; take joy in the day the Lord hath made. For God has said you will "undergo many trials in this life"; the trials you face are not to harm you but to give you hope.

Whatever difficulties challenge you, ask Jesus to help you see things the way He sees them, and consider it an opportunity to grow in your faith. Do what you can and leave the rest to Him. Trust in Him always! Be sober and alert for the time will be soon, then you will overcome, and God will use them for the good.

Therefore, be joyful for this day and for God's protection.

Do you remember a difficult time when God helped you grow in faith and gave you hope?

In your *Becoming Anchored Companion Journal*, use the prompts and space for your reflections.

Thoughts:

_____

_____

_____

_____

_____

_____

_____

_____

_____

_____

_____

_____

Prayer:

_____

_____

_____

_____

_____

_____

_____

_____

_____

WEEK 41

Don't be afraid, for I am with you. Don't be discouraged, for I am your God. I will strengthen you and help you. I will hold you up with my victorious right hand.
Isaiah 41:10 (NLT)

A nxiety and stress are draining, but the Lord will restore you when you focus on Him and not yourself. We hope to be strong, courageous, and wise. By ourselves our resources are limited, but with God all things are possible. Ask God to help you overcome your obstacles and thank Him for all He has done. The first step is to believe!

As you age, you may have regrets that follow, a lost opportunity, relationship, even your will to live life joyfully. I have learned we keep growing when we keep learning. With God, you can start over. God may have something better in mind for you; maybe that is why you have been struggling. Keep your hope alive and believe all things are possible with God!

Does your hope begin with you or with God?

Do you remember a time God gave you the resources to rise?

In your *Becoming Anchored Companion Journal,* use the prompts and space for your reflections.

Thoughts:

_____

_____

_____

_____

_____

_____

_____

_____

_____

_____

_____

Prayer:

_____

_____

_____

_____

_____

_____

_____

_____

_____

WEEK 42

We believe it is through the grace of our Lord Jesus that we are saved, just as they are.
Acts 15:11 (NIV)

S ometimes I listen to inspirational and motivational audiobooks. The author is usually engaging and knows how to grab attention. I find these books challenge my thoughts and inspire new ideas and thought patterns. I find this helpful when I want to learn more about what interests me and aligns with God's purposes. The same holds true when reading Scripture. It is inspiring and we learn how others have gone through everything we do, and how God's grace has been a lifeline to many, which gives us hope.

How does Jesus influence your thoughts?

Who else has inspired you?

What do you hope for?

In your *Becoming Anchored Companion Journal,* use the prompts and space for your reflections.

Thoughts:

_____

_____

_____

_____

_____

_____

_____

_____

_____

_____

Prayer:

_____

_____

_____

_____

_____

_____

_____

_____

_____

WEEK 43

But as a mountain erodes and crumbles and as a rock is moved from its place, as water wears away stones and torrents wash away the soil, so you destroy a person's hope.
Job 14:18-19 (NIV)

Unfortunately, too many are led astray by words, often hurtful. We are called to be steadfast, for the Word of God alone does not permit others to condemn one another. Be inspiring; encourage others like Barnabas, Paul's mentor in Acts!

If you need help, remember this acronym for THINK: "True, Helpful, Inspiring, Necessary, Kind".

I pray Lord Jesus my words would be kind and inspiring to others. So I ask, please speak through me so my words are helpful and encouraging, in Jesus' name, Amen.

In what ways do you inspire people and give them hope?

In your *Becoming Anchored Companion Journal,* use the prompts and space for your reflections.

Thoughts:

_____

_____

_____

_____

_____

_____

_____

_____

_____

_____

_____

Prayer:

_____

_____

_____

_____

_____

_____

_____

_____

_____

_____

_____

WEEK 44

Our great desire is that you will keep on loving others as long as life lasts, in order to make certain that what you hope for will come true.
Hebrews 6:11 (NLT)

When others notice your steadfast Faith, one of two things begin to happen. Blessings begin to flow into your life or theirs. Paul is asking us to be patient upon the Lord. God wants to see how obedient you are towards His decrees and to praise Him while you wait. Be joyful and express your gratitude.

Finding acceptance is also an act of love, for if you do love someone, they may not always meet your expectations. You may not always get what you want from a relationship, but you don't want to burn any bridges either.

Has your Faith encouraged someone you know?

Do you remain hopeful for your dreams to come to fruition?

In your *Becoming Anchored Companion Journal,* use the prompts and space for your reflections.

Thoughts:

_____

_____

_____

_____

_____

_____

_____

_____

_____

_____

Prayer:

_____

_____

_____

_____

_____

_____

_____

_____

_____

WEEK 45

Blessed is the one who perseveres under trial because, having stood the test, that person will receive the crown of life that the Lord has promised to those who love him.
James 1:12 (NIV)

Too often when adversity strikes, we tend to feel uncertain, hopeless, and powerless. When we discover the power of letting go and letting God into every aspect of our lives, blessings begin to follow.

Many of us know that life can be stressful if we let it. There are ways to relieve that stress through self-care. Taking a walk, a hobby, talking with a friend are a few ways to destress. When we step back for a minute, we may gain a new perspective. For myself, prayer helps me regain my focus on what truly matters most in my life at the moment.

See what works for you.

How does this Bible verse give you hope?

In your *Becoming Anchored Companion Journal,* use the prompts and space for your reflections.

Thoughts:

_____

_____

_____

_____

_____

_____

_____

_____

_____

_____

Prayer:

_____

_____

_____

_____

_____

_____

_____

_____

_____

_____

WEEK 46

You are my refuge and my shield; your word is my source of hope.
Psalms 119:114 (NLT)

Too often when looking for comfort in other people, we are essentially placing them above God. Soon we will be disappointed when they don't meet our expectations and we feel hopeless. While we can find satisfaction in other people, having hopes they will be our source of happiness will end up letting us down eventually.

Consider turning to God. He is the only true source of our happiness. We know this by His promises, such as the Bible verse here in Psalm 119. We can come to the realization that God is really our only true source of Joy and is our harbor.

Have you anchored your source of hope with God?

In what ways has He provided protection for you when you sought refuge with Him?

In your *Becoming Anchored Companion Journal*, use the prompts and space for your reflections.

Thoughts:

_____

_____

_____

_____

_____

_____

_____

_____

_____

_____

_____

Prayer:

_____

_____

_____

_____

_____

_____

_____

_____

_____

_____

WEEK 47

Jesus said to His followers, "Because of this, I say to you, do not worry about your life, what you are going to eat. Do not worry about your body, what you are going to wear."
Luke 12:22 (NLV)

G od's grace is good for today. We really don't know what's going to happen tomorrow. Now, while it's fine to plan ahead, today is today and we should live to the fullest every moment of every day.

Therefore, our hope is with the Lord. He will supply us with our needs every day, one day at a time. When I was younger, starting out as a contractor running my own business, I was obsessed with planning, worrying, and always thinking of tomorrow. Well, tomorrow came again and again, but I missed many todays.

How about you? Are you hoping for a better tomorrow or are you living today?

In your *Becoming Anchored Companion Journal,* use the prompts and space for your reflections.

Thoughts:

_____

_____

_____

_____

_____

_____

_____

_____

_____

_____

_____

Prayer:

_____

_____

_____

_____

_____

_____

_____

_____

_____

_____

WEEK 48

And now, Lord, what do I wait for? My Hope is in you.
Psalm 39:7 (NKJV)

I enjoy the summer months lounging by the pool or gazing out at the lake while boaters take advantage of boating season here in Michigan. Our summers are short in contrast to Florida. However, we spend our time wisely during the summer and don't take it for granted because here in Michigan, the splendid fall colors will be upon us quickly. I love seeing the reflections off the lakes or taking color tours by car. Autumn has lots to offer and give thanks for while preparing for yet another season. Winter and then spring again.

Maybe you're going through a difficult season now. In what season do you find your hope?

How can you begin to turn to God in all seasons and let Him be your hope no matter your circumstances?

In your *Becoming Anchored Companion Journal*, use the prompts and space for your reflections.

Thoughts:

_____

_____

_____

_____

_____

_____

_____

_____

_____

_____

_____

_____

Prayer:

_____

_____

_____

_____

_____

_____

_____

_____

_____

_____

WEEK 49

Delight yourself also in the Lord, and He shall give you the desires of your heart.
Psalm 37:4 (NIV)

Searching for your purpose can be overwhelming and terrifying. You might ask, "What if my desires don't come to light?" Well let me tell you this, my friend. God cares more about what's in your heart. So, think of it like this. Do your desires align with God's purpose for you? How do you know for sure? What do you enjoy doing more than anything?

Get to know God better, through prayer, scripture, and meditation. Seek Him with all your heart. Do not lean on your own understanding. Proverbs 3:5 (NKJV)

Know what pleases God and what God detests.

Do your desires please God or yourself?

In your *Becoming Anchored Companion Journal,* use the prompts and space for your reflections.

Thoughts:

_____
_____
_____
_____
_____
_____
_____
_____
_____
_____
_____

Prayer:

_____
_____
_____
_____
_____
_____
_____
_____
_____
_____

WEEK 50

Perseverance, character; and character, hope.
Romans 5:4 (NIV)

In Romans 5, it is further stated that through our sorrows brings perseverance. Paul had mentioned in Philippians how he pressed on and moved forward. Life goes on, as they say. And so, it does!

Do everything to bring glory to God. For through our sorrows, we hope to be of help to others who are going through the same circumstances we have. All through the Bible, it speaks of how one person went through difficult times and of those who sought hope in the Lord who then brought them through their trials.

Job lost everything he owned, everyone he loved.

Joseph was scared of what folks would think when Mary was impregnated by the Holy Spirit.

Jesus was crucified for our sins.

How does your perseverance reveal your character and where your hope lies?

In your *Becoming Anchored Companion Journal,* use the prompts and space for your reflections.

Thoughts:

_____

_____

_____

_____

_____

_____

_____

_____

_____

_____

_____

Prayer:

_____

_____

_____

_____

_____

_____

_____

_____

_____

WEEK 51

Rejoice in our confident hope, be patient in trouble, and keep on praying.
Romans 12:12 (NLV)

My favorite passage in the entire Bible is Romans 12! Paul teaches us how to live a righteous life to the fullest. The Psalmist also says to wait patiently upon the Lord. We know this to be certain when we hope and wait patiently upon the Lord, knowing He will direct our paths, be our refuge and strength, our source of love and comfort. For only God is our source from where everything comes from and goes. He is the Alpha and the Omega.

When you live an obedient life, you'll experience His Peace transcending through you to live in harmony with Him. This is my hope, and my hope for you.

Be still and know that I am God. The one with whom all blessings flow.

What is your hope?

How does your life illuminate peace?

In your *Becoming Anchored Companion Journal,* use the prompts and space for your reflections.

Thoughts:

_____

_____

_____

_____

_____

_____

_____

_____

_____

_____

_____

Prayer:

_____

_____

_____

_____

_____

_____

_____

_____

_____

WEEK 52

And we know God causes everything to work together for the good of those who
Love God and are called according to His purpose.
Romans 8:28 (NIV)

I f you have chosen to live according to God and His will as I have,
you too will experience His Peace. What more may we hope for:
Live in peace, in harmony with others, and with God. He will move
mountains for you, so you may live with expectancy of all good
things to come. He hopes you will share your blessings with others.
He will make your paths straight and make your enemies a footstool
for your feet. "Do not take matters into your own hand," declares
the Lord, but let Him take revenge.

Dear God, I pray this day and for the days to come, that you
would teach me your decrees and use me to help others with the gifts
you have bestowed upon me. Thank you for your grace, mercy, and
love. Your peace that surpasses anything I have ever experienced or
hoped for. Thank you for the joy that each new day brings. In Jesus'
name, Amen.

How is God working in your life?
Have you chosen to live in harmony with others and with
God?

In your *Becoming Anchored Companion Journal,* use the prompts and
space for your reflections.

Thoughts:

_____

_____

_____

_____

_____

_____

_____

_____

_____

_____

Prayer:

_____

_____

_____

_____

_____

_____

_____

_____

_____

_____

ADDITIONAL RESOURCES

If you haven't yet, I encourage you to get the *Becoming Anchored Companion Journal* to dig deeper as you grow in hope, faith, and trust in the Lord. Get the free PDF at:. thomasbrattonauthor.com/becoming-anchored-gift

Follow me for updates concerning upcoming devotionals and other resources.

Follow me on Facebook:
https://www.facebook.com/3Pslivinnow

Follow me on Instagram:
https://www.instagram.com/thomas_bratton_author

Follow me on LinkedIn:
https://www.linkedin.com/in/thomas-bratton-baab9244

Follow me on Pinterest:
https://www.pinterest.com/becominganchoredtb

Follow me on Goodreads:
https://www.goodreads.com/author/show/22971770.Thoma s_Bratton

Visit my website and encouraging blog:
https://thomasbrattonauthor.com

THANK YOU!

Thank you so much for taking the time to read the *Becoming Anchored* weekly devotional. I hope you found it immensely beneficial in your spiritual journey. Know as you go through life how precious you are to God, for He loves you.

I am grateful to all whom supported me and my endeavor during my writings, and to my writing coach, Katelyn Silva, for her enthusiasm and guidance. I would also like to thank my wife, Gina Bratton, for her love and encouragement to finish this devotional.

To my Mom and Dad who passed before I finished writing. It is through their values and love for family I adhere to a life of family, friends and service with the utmost integrity and love for God.

Would you take a moment and leave an honest review on the author page? It would mean so much to me and help get the devotional in the hands of others who would find it valuable.

amazon.com/author/becominganchoredthomasbratton

goodreads.com/book/show/63047132-becoming-anchored

barnesandnoble.com/w/becoming-anchored-thomas-bratton/1142648063?ean=9798985916546